Are you looking for love that is genuine? Are you looking for a lover that will encourage, comfort, and consol you when every area of your life seems so fragile? Do you want to know how to wait on the one who will love you back for who you are and not what you have? Have you ever wondered what it truly means to embrace love with your soul and not with your flesh?

Every woman is a divine masterpiece fashioned in the hands of her true and everlasting lover. He will never leave you nor forsake you. He will be right there with you holding your hand at every momentous occasion and every pain piercing moment. Jesus, the one true love that is guaranteed, will teach you how to overcome with joy, peace, and passion as you seek his face to discern his soft and gentle voice to know Him in a very real way.

As you read through every vignette, let your soul ponder and your heart heal, as you come along side Leah Savage as she guides you on a journey of how to draw from Loves deep waters to arrive at your own personal moment of being Married To Love.

A wife. A mother. A sister. A friend. A daughter and a woman of God. Uniquely elegant and simply beautiful.
-Your Sister, Lillian

Leah Savage speaks with a strength that is rare to find these days. She equally wields truth and courage as she speaks from the heart with love. Well-versed on issues ranging from social justice to spiritual endurance and perseverance in dark times, this is an author you will not soon forget, and whose perspective you will come to value and trust.
-Your Sister, Portia

Married
to
Love

Leah Cherice Savage

Married To Love

iUniverse books may be ordered through booksellers or by contacting:

iUniverse
1663 Liberty Drive
Bloomington, IN 47403
www.iuniverse.com
1-800-Authors (1-800-288-4677)

ISBN: 978-1-4401-6484-2 (sc)

Print information available on the last page.

iUniverse rev. date: 3/28/2015

Table of Contents

In loving memory of my grandmother Grace W. Perkins,
who gave me an example of a Proverbs 31 woman.
Grandma, I love you and I miss you.

In loving memory of Mama Keitt,
who made sure that I knew that
she loved me through her giving spirit,
her gentle hugs, and her priceless wisdom.
Mama Keitt, thank you for inspiring me to love others as you
loved me.

To my mother:
Mrs. Arabelle Louise Jackson,
whose love has anchored me
since the time that I was a little girl,
Cherishing your love in my heart Mama Eagle, I am now flying.

To my father:
Mr. Frank Lee Jackson, I love you daddy. I know you're proud.

To my mother-in-love: Mama Shirley, whose love has been
tangible and real,
Mom I love you and thank you for loving me from your heart,
beyond words, and with your actions.

To Dad Savage and Mom Lynn, you have embraced me as your
daughter and I love you both. Your support has comforted me and
encouraged me. Thank you with all my heart.

To my sisters and aunts in Christ, whose love and prayers have comforted me in the dark hours and rejoiced with me upon the rising of the Son. I love each of you by name: Monique, Natasha, Rissa, Regina, Kimberly, Portia, Kelly, Shabby, Eustacia, Ashleigh, Danielle, Melissa, Auntie Evelyn, Auntie Yvette, Aunt Tamara, Auntie Karen, Auntie Yolanda, Aunt Lois, Nana Ruby, Lillian, Heather, and to my countless sisters, aunts and cousins from past to present to future.

To my daughter, Miquela Cherice Savage, who is the manifestation of your mommy and daddy's love. I love you "Mama" and my greatest desire for you is to be in love with Jesus. To my son, Elisha Lee Savage, you have my heart "little man". I love you.

To my husband, whose love has propelled me into my destiny, and unveiled the princess that was hidden within; You are the most beautiful manifestation of Love in my life. John, I love you with all that I am and all that I ever will be.

To my Husband and Lord for eternity, Lord Jesus, without you there would be nothing to write about. I love you with my very breath. Be glorified through the words in these pages.

Prologue

In the silence of solitude, Love spoke to me. He said: "I love you. I will help you to sleep. I will help you to eat." Love-a word that comes and goes. But who really knows what it means to really love someone?

Upon reflection of life, namely my life, I've seen many things during these last and evil days. I've seen war, natural disasters, poverty, destruction, hearts crying because of broken promises and unfulfilled dreams. And upon deeper introspection, I've seen my internal wars, the disasters within, my spiritual and emotional poverty, destruction of my innocence, my own weeping, broken heart bleeding from things almost too painful to mention. And yet, in the pain of silence, my hushed screams, my cries of internal anguish, my quiet desperation, I have not given up. I've refused to give up. I won't give up. I can't give up. Why do I see a reason to bear with the pain of this world any longer?

Because I am married to Love. Who is Love? My Lord and Savior Jesus Christ. He is Love, and like the song says: "Love lifted me, when nothing else could help, love lifted me."

My marriage to Love has been a process, a journey from birth until now. Love knew me before the creation of the world, and His purposes for me have just begun to unfold.

Come with me as I reflect upon my relationship with my Husband, Love. This is not meant to be a blueprint for your life. It's a testimony of what Love will do if you let Him in your life. He has a special love just for you. This is my love story, and I pray that it will inspire you to let Love write a story of you and Him that is all your own.

"Love at First Sight"

*Here I am! I stand at the door and knock. If anyone
hears my voice and opens the door, I will come in and
eat with him, and he with me. Revelation 3:20*

During the summer of 1987, I was seven years old.
The oldest child with a two year old sister, my identity had
already begun to emerge. I helped out with my little sister
and did whatever my mom and dad needed me to do. My
quiet, introspective nature, led me along softly, quietly, ever
so gently.

At this point in my young life, I was just beginning to
know Love. I attended church with my family since birth. I
heard sermons, attended Sunday school. I spent much of the
time writing notes on the front pew. Blah, blah, blah. I heard
His name: Jesus Christ. What did He have for me? What did
He want from me? What did I have for Him?

And then it happened, gradually, slowly, in the fullness of
time. Love drew me to Himself.

For three weeks I heard His voice in my little spirit. Every time the pastor gave the invitation to accept Christ, I wanted to come. But I was afraid; afraid of all those adults looking at me. Life was "fine" without Jesus, or so I thought. How would my life change? Fear began his purpose of keeping me away from Love on that day. Yet, the wooing of Love was stronger than fear could ever be. On the third call, three weeks later, I came. It was the most important decision I have ever made. I walked down the aisle and met Love: Jesus the Christ. I professed Him as my Lord and Savior.

The pastor of my church at the time, New Testament Baptist Church, explained the plan of salvation to me. He took me to the scriptures in Romans 10:9-11 and John 3:16. He told me that man is separated from God because of our sin. In order to reconcile man to Himself God came to earth in the body of Jesus and died on a cross at a place called Calvary. Jesus was sacrificed for my sins, and rose from the dead, with the gift of eternal life for all those who believe in Him. Because I had heard my pastor share these ideas many times, I shook my head in agreement. I confessed with my mouth that Jesus is the Lord God Himself. I believed in my heart that God raised Jesus from the dead, and I agreed to be baptized shortly thereafter. I was told that Baptism is symbolic of Jesus' death at Calvary. Just as Jesus died in His body, I too would be immersed into the baptismal waters and die to my "flesh". Just as Jesus rose from death to life, I too would emerge from the baptismal waters into a new life, a new spirit. I would be reborn and become a child of God!

On September 7, 1987, I was baptized, and truly "born again" in my spirit as God's daughter. When my body came up from that cold baptism water, something had changed. I felt clean throughout my entire inner self. Joy and peace and righteousness entered my heart, mind and spirit. On that day, I could feel the warmth of God through His Son and His Holy Spirit, radiating on my face, from the inside out. Love had cleansed me through and through with His blood.

From then on, our journey began. Love and I intertwined to become Beloved and Sacred Lover. Yes, *He* loved me at first sight.

"In This is Love"

*This is love: not that we loved God, but that He loved us
and sent His Son as an atoning sacrifice for our sins.
I John 4:10*

Have you ever loved someone and they hardly ever spoke
to you? How painful! How seemingly tragic to love someone
without being loved in return. So it was for the first five years
of my relationship with Jesus. He loved me consistently. Every
need I had, He supplied. I babysat every weekend, earning
enough to sustain my ten year old needs and wants. My
mother taught me to give Jesus ten percent of what I earned.
I recall those Sundays when I got home from church, after I
had put in my one or two dollar tithes and the phone rang. It
was another babysitting job awaiting my acceptance. Oh how
sweet, it was to obey the words of my Lord and Savior!

I prayed to Him, went to church, but did my commitment
match His sacrifice? His unfailing love? His yearning for
me? Every morning He gave me breath. He woke me up

with shelter, warmth, food and clothing. My body was never violated. He protected my virginity from being touched. He dried my tears. He loved the *me* inside of me that no one else could see. His grace, mercy, forgiveness picked me up each time I fell from His perfect will.

In this is love: not that I, Leah Cherice Savage, loved God, but that He loved me.

His love was and is matchless and perfect; selfless and eternal. *He* was and is the anchor of my soul.

During those silent years when I was just beginning to learn what it meant to pray, He still loved me.   He held me and rocked me to sleep each night. He caused the sun to shine on my dark days. He put a rainbow in my clouds. Love was tender, patient, and longsuffering with me. His heart longed for my presence, simply that He might love me, be with me, talk to me, and care for me. If only I knew what I had. If I knew that I was *so* loved, perhaps the years to come would have seen less tears.

Time passed, and I began to call on Love. I needed Him. It was time to go deeper and higher.

In this is love.

I Cried for Love

"And anyone who does not take his cross and follow me is not worthy of me. Whoever finds his life will lose it, and whoever loses his life for my sake, will find it"
Matthew 10:38-39

It was September 1993, and eighth grade awaited me. I had only a few friends, but my most faithful "friend" was solitude. Solitude and I have kept each other company for years. This year, we became especially close.

Why was this year so sad for me? Why did I feel so alone? It was Love. Not everyone knew Love at my school, or my church for that matter. I couldn't just hang out with everyone and do what everyone else did. Love called me higher.

But there was a price I had to pay to be friends with Love. I made a choice not to simply "hang out" during my lunchtimes. At the onset of adolescence, I was struggling to define myself, deconstruct my world, and answer the questions: "Who am I?" and "To whom do I belong?" I wanted purposeful, meaningful relationships. Love kept calling my name, summoning me to go higher. But the higher I got, the lonelier I became. Was Love worth it? I cried. I wept.

All I wanted was true friendship. Love opened the door of my heart for a few to come in, but I couldn't hold on to them too tight. Jesus wanted to be first in my life. He paid the price for me, first at Calvary. Then during those first five years of our relationship, His yearning for intimacy drew me near. Now, was the time for me to pick up my cross, and follow Love into a place He would show me.

I remember telling myself over and over again that I would trust in the Lord with all of my heart, in the midst of the tears that flowed down my face.

No matter the cost, I chose Love. Love knelt down to where I was. Jesus cared enough to dry every tear that fell from my eyes.

There is a loneliness that can be rocked. Love rocked me. Jesus spoke to me in the silence of solitude. Love heard my cries. At first they were hopeless, and then my heart made a vow to take up my cross and follow Jesus, even when the cost felt great.

My vow to Love:

"When time has stolen away our stars and

Only the night endures,

Yet somewhere in the darkness, Love,

My hand will still seek yours,

When youth has danced its parting dance

And tasted its last sweet wine, yet somewhere in

The silence Love, your hand will still find mine"

Thomas Kinkade

I cried for Love.

Love Spoke Calvary

"But he said to me, "My grace is sufficient for you, for my power is made perfect in weakness. Therefore I will boast all the more gladly about my weaknesses, so that Christ's power may rest on me"
2 Corinthians 12:9

I knew with my mind that Jesus loved me. I knew that I was forgiven for my sins. I knew that I was cleansed by the blood of the Lamb that was slain.

But I didn't *really* believe any of these things *in my heart*. It was my heart that mattered, for as a man thinks in his heart, so is he (Proverbs 23:7a).

Even at thirteen, I had a deposit of lies that I already believed in my heart, which corrupted my thinking. I was afraid of sinning in the most shameful ways. One fear haunted me from age thirteen until I was eighteen.

11

I couldn't even tell anyone how I felt. I just held it close to my heart. It tried to choke the seed of love planted therein. Until Jesus came in.

At the verge of a breakdown when I was thirteen because of the fear that tormented me, in my mind's eye I saw a cross; I heard the three most powerful words I have ever heard: "I love you."

The weight of my fear fell as a river of tears streamed from my eyes. I could see the cross, the blood, Jesus' arms stretched out wide to hold me, *me.*

From that point on, Love was real.

Jesus was and is more than a man, God, creator, or Son of God. He was and still is my Friend. The Friend I had always longed for. He shattered my loneliness. Jesus is real, the image of the invisible God. He promised me love, *real* love. His love set me free.

I was free, *finally*, and I could say at last "Love lifted me, when *nothing* else could help, Jesus lifted me."

Jesus is the true Lover of my soul, the one and only God incarnate.

No longer did I cry for the wings of a dove, to fly away and be at rest. In the middle of my circumstances, in God's arms, my soul found her eternal rest. Like the Israelites in the Old Testament, my time in Egypt was over.

Love spoke Calvary.

Love Chose Me

*"You did not choose me, but I chose you and appointed you
to go and bear fruit-fruit that will last. Then the Father
will give you whatever you ask in my name"*
John 15:16

Why does it always seem that the one person you love,
the one person your heart chooses doesn't love you in return?
Such was my case anywhere from age 13 and beyond. Those
men whose love was unrequited are beautiful children of God.
My prayer is that God would bless them, because they deeply
blessed my life. How can unrequited love reap deep blessings?
Through years of experience, I have learned the bittersweet
plight of my best Friend, Love. To love completely regardless
of whether you are loved in return: this is the plight of Love.

"In this is love, not that we loved God, but that He loved us
and sent His Son to be the propitiation for our sins. Beloved,
if God so loved us, we ought also to love one another" I John
4:10.

Throughout adolescence, I learned the sting of rejection, and how the heart of the lover breaks silently, slowly and softly when love is not reciprocated. Yet the sweetest lesson I have gained is the awareness that Love *chose me*. God gives each man the free will to love Him or not. In perfect love we each have a choice to make. Because Love chose me, I choose Him daily.

When I hated God and forsook Him; when I rejected, crucified, beat Jesus with my sins, He loved me. It didn't matter if I was pretty or small enough, light, dark or talented enough, He loved me. He loves me simply because He is Love. His love isn't selfish, but it is selfless, patient, kind, unfailing, eternal, matchless and true. In the eyes of Love, I am His beloved, chosen, fearfully and wonderfully made, just as I am. Love chose me.

Love Overflowed Me

*"You prepare a table before me in the presence of my
enemies. You anoint my head with oil; my cup overflows.
Surely goodness and love will follow me all the days of my
life, and I will dwell in the house of the Lord forever"*
Psalms 23:5-6

My cup ran over during my sophomore year in high school.
It was time for me to begin again, again. I had moved from
one side of Sacramento to another at the end of my freshman
year. Was I sad? No, I was delighted! I could say goodbye to
the pain of those few years on that side of town. I could start
afresh, anew. I could possibly make another friend to add to
my Friendship with Love.

What happened my sophomore year? Love overflowed
me. I couldn't even count my blessings because they were so
numerous. The most beautiful gift Love gave me was a voice
and a purpose to speak on His behalf. I gave a speech He had
given me about Affirmative Action. At its heart, the speech

was really about justice and equality; opportunity and hope for those dearest to my heart: those discriminated against and marginalized within society.

Love paved my way through a very special person in my life so that I would speak in Sacramento and be flown as a sixteen year old speaker to a Los Angeles Bar Association Luncheon. What did I do to receive such treatment at such a young age? Love didn't look at my age, but like David, Joseph, and Mary in the Bible, He saw my potential to bear fruit, *much* fruit that would last. I spoke with all of my heart and captivated the hearts and minds of others. It was my season of blessings. Showers of blessings overtook me. I smiled and I knew the sorrow of my yesteryears no more. For a moment, the enemy of my soul left me alone. None of his devices could keep Love from blessing me or snatch me from Love's hand. Love overflowed me.

Love Gave Me a Moment

*"The eyes of all look to you, and you give them their food at
the proper time. You open your hand and satisfy the desires
of every living thing"
Psalms 145:15-16*

A moment: usually it doesn't last long. Yet, it can be a
powerful, poignant testimony to the workings of Love.

In February 1998, I was still single. I felt all alone. I had
resigned myself to being single for as long as I could see into the
future. All I had known was letting go. But then he came.

My first boyfriend came into my life. It was truly like a
fairytale. He called me without fail every Sunday. He treated
me like I was beautiful. Me? Beautiful? He took me out and
paid for all of my meals, like I was to be nourished with the
finest foods. He shivered when *I* was cold, as if he could feel
the beating of my heart and the coldness in my hands. What
he really did for me was to show me that I was worthy to be
loved and to be held, and to be *wanted*, not just needed.

He was an extension of Love. Love held me tight with *his* arms. Love wrote me the sweetest poetry with *his* pen. Love brought out a side of me that had been hurt and hidden, through *his* touch. Love looked me in the eye and revealed the content of His soul, through this young man's gaze.

Though it ended, because I obeyed the voice of Love telling me to end it, Love had given me a moment.

Price of Love

"If anyone comes to me and does not hate his father and mother, his wife and children, his brothers and sisters-yes, even his own life-he cannot be my disciple"
Luke 14:26

As I walked up to the podium, thoughts rushed through my mind. "Did I give enough? Was I too closed, too guarded? Did I rob myself and others of the fruit of friendship, the priceless pearls of relationship?"

In June of 1998, I was one of my high schools' three valedictorians. My portion of the speech we gave together resounded with a call to service. As high school graduates, now was the moment of decision, I proclaimed. Would we serve our fellowman or seek to "get ours?"

But as I gave my speech, I wondered if I had served my peers during high school when I had the chance? As I spoke, everyone seemed like a grain of sand in the sea of faces. I didn't even *really* know anyone. After four years, I felt so empty, so friendless. How could I reconcile what I was saying with how I had lived my life up until that point? When commencement ceremonies were over, I went home and Love spoke. Surrounding me at home were the relationships in which I had been touched and those I had touched. I looked at my mom and dad, my little sister and my closest girlfriends. I looked with love upon the face of my spiritual grandmother, Mama Keitt, who has since gone home to be with the Lord. All around me were my relatives, each of whom I love dearly.

Then I knew the answer. I *had* given, loved and opened my heart to receive and be loved. Though the number of people my heart had invited in was small, they were all hand chosen by Love. Love taught me to befriend most everyone I met. But Love only allowed a special few to enter those secret places of my heart. My heart was too tender, too fragile and too easily broken. I couldn't just let anyone and everyone in. The price I paid to be close to Love was actually His protection of me.

At the end of those high school years, Love was first. No earthly person could fulfill my need for the divine Creator. Jesus was and still is my Savior *and* Lord, and just as He reigned in *every* area of my life then, He reigns in my life now.

The price of Love.

Consuming Fire of Love

"See I have refined you, though not as silver; I have tested you in the furnace of affliction. For my own sake, for my own sake, I do this. How can I let myself be defamed? I will not yield my glory to another"
Isaiah 48:10-11

It truly was a dream come true, a vision made manifest. After four years of working diligently and envisioning myself at Stanford University, I was there. The whole world seemed to be at the tip of my grasp. The special young man I became close to in high school was still a part of my life. I told myself that I would "believe" Love for a change, and stop worrying about my life. I had scholarships and the support of family and friends who wanted nothing, but for me to succeed.

So what could happen to obstruct my picture of perfection? Hadn't I paid my dues and now my life would just ebb and flow at my every whim and fancy? Oh, but Love, Jesus the Christ had another idea, a better plan.

He shook my world and consumed me with His love.

I gave up the only boyfriend I had ever known, because Jesus was my first Love and I chose to obey His call for time alone with me. I faced the uncertainty of not having enough money to pay for Stanford. I began to see the *me* inside of me that sent Jesus to the cross. Visions of my pride and perfection, doubt and anxiety, worry, fear, and unbelief sent me into months of depression. I hated myself and didn't even want to eat.

I began to re-live childhood fears and childhood pains. The sorrow was so great that like the Psalmist in Psalm 42, my tears became my food. I had to deal with hidden emotions, hidden feelings that rose to the surface, all illuminated by the Word of God.

Like Paul, the New Testament apostle, I didn't do the good I wanted to do, but I did the evil I didn't want to do.

For years I learned to control my outward behavior, but I couldn't control my unruly, unpredictable broken heart. I had been raised in the church. How could I have such debased and ungodly thoughts? For a year, I wrestled with my feelings. Love was ever so patient with me. The lessons I was to learn were so simple, but they required a sacrifice, a cost which seemed almost impossible to pay. I made my learning process harder and more complicated because of my "Type A", obsessive compulsive personality tendencies. But Love wasn't worried. He knew the truth.

Jesus died to set me free from *all* of my sins. At the cross, all sin and shame are cleansed by the blood of the Lamb, my Savior, and Love. What I had to do was *really* believe in my heart that I was forgiven. I had to forgive others as I had been forgiven. I had to realize that at Calvary *all was finished*. Most importantly, I had to learn to let go.

Love held my hand through it all. In fact, He held me in His arms. As a Father chastening His beloved child, He chastened me. As a mother comforts her baby, so my Heavenly Father comforted me. His consuming fire refined me into pure gold. And over time, I saw the truth and I believed it, and it set me free. Indeed, I was free. On the surface, it looked like Love hated me, because of the pain and the sorrow. The fire of my circumstances and the wind of the Spirit shook the foundation of my past, and set my feet again on the solid Rock of Jesus Christ. Now I know, as I look back, that it was the sin in me that Love hated, and as a Consuming Fire, He set me free. "Therefore if the Son makes you free, you shall be free indeed" John 8:36.

"Jesus Makes It Sweet"

In the bitter waters of life that flood the depths of my soul,

Oh sweet Jesus, You fill me with Your love, You melt and make me whole.

Jesus makes it sweet.

Those bitter tears that fall from my eyes, my burdened and heavy cries, fall from my head to my feet.

Oh, Jesus makes it sweet.

I praise You, for Your power has conquered the chains of my sin, because of You, this race I win.

Bitterness. Pain. Heartache. Sickness. Toil. Strife and Defeat.

Jesus, You make it sweet.

A Vision of Innocence Conceived by Love

*"Therefore, whoever humbles himself like this child is the
greatest in the kingdom of heaven."*
Matthew 18:4

On my nineteenth birthday, I awoke with no idea of what
to expect. I really wasn't trying to celebrate another year of
my life. Though my freshman year of college was a time of
immense growth and my character was refined by the fires of
life, I was left with a wounded, desolate feeling.

Like one who has endured a battle, I had been attacked,
mentally, physically, spiritually and emotionally. My body
shook with anemia and my mind was exhausted after battling
thoughts of sin and death. I felt perpetually tired. I had made
it, but I felt more like a survivor than a conqueror, let alone
more than a conqueror.

I woke up to another year of anticipated heartache. Would 19 be as hard as 18? I wondered. And then Love touched me. Gently, quietly, softly, He spoke.

My mom brought to me my birthday presents that morning: stationary, envelopes, and a book entitled **Woman Thou Art Loosed**, by Bishop T.D. Jakes. When I saw that book, something broke free inside of me. Me, loosed? I asked. What really brought me tears of joy was that my daddy bought me that book. He was the source of much of my deep-felt emotions of love and pain. It was as if he was setting his *big girl* free just by giving me that book.

And so, on my nineteenth birthday, I cried. Tears of healing, joy and freedom, poured forth from my wounded heart. Love spoke calm to my storm. It was over, finally. My sins had been paid for at Calvary. He reminded me at that moment that it was finished at the cross, and I could celebrate my birthday, my life, without hopeless resignation or sorrow.

My desolation still remained, though. I had given up a man who actually loved me. I had learned what it really means to trust God when you can't see your way. Love literally carried me through. When I didn't want to eat, Love was there to walk me to the dining hall. He gave me the strength to put the food I didn't desire on my tray. He walked with me back to my room, when everyone else was gone. I had reached a point when sleep wasn't even peaceful. Tormenting thoughts and dreams from satan tried to destroy my sanity. I learned in those moments, just how fierce my enemy was. His sole purpose was to kill my hope, steal my joy, and destroy me.

Many times, it seemed like he was on the verge of victory. Thoughts of suicide took hold of me, and I longed for death more than I wanted life. But, my song wasn't meant to end. My enemy had been, scorned, shamed and destroyed at the cross of Jesus (Colossians 2:15). Love was stronger than my hopelessness. He remained in control throughout my entire freshman year.

As I sat there on my birthday in my bed, memories of my moments with Jesus flooded my mind. The enemy didn't want my story to pass on, but it has. I am here, victorious and alive; at peace, beloved, and much more than a conqueror!

That summer, Love gave me a vision of myself as a little girl. Before this summer, I saw myself as a lonely young woman longing for more than I had. I had entertained the idealism of perfection, but found it to be an empty goal, bankrupt, devoid of purpose, hope and meaning. That idol died in 1998-1999. My world of outward perfection was shattered and I saw the true contents of my heart. I died that year, only to live again.

On July 16, 1999 the Lord gave me a vision of myself as a little girl, full of hope, truly able to rejoice in the times to come. Love held me in His arms, like a daddy cradling his little girl. Jesus restored my innocence, which the enemy robbed from me. Love even called me beautiful. He called me worthy of love, chosen and not forsaken, beloved and not unloved, full and not empty, surrounded and not alone.

In time, I would believe these truths. In time, I would walk in my vision of innocence, conceived by Love.

No Longer Empty, but in Love

"Jesus answered, 'Everyone who drinks this water will be
thirsty again, but whoever drinks the water I give him will
never thirst. Indeed, the water I give him will become in
him a spring of water welling up to eternal life"
John 4:13

After a fire, the earth is left barren, desolate, and empty. Such was my state as I prepared to return to Stanford my sophomore year. The fire of my freshman year refined parts of me that I didn't know existed, and now I was left with the remnants of a broken and contrite spirit; the remnants of my heart, my mind, my purpose for life, and my passion for living. I had vowed to myself and to Love that this year I would eat and nurture my temple, the body I had been given. It was time to start thinking about a major, but what I really wanted was time; time to heal.

As I searched my soul throughout that year, I found the essence of my longings. I didn't care about perfection anymore, and I was tired of being lonely. I longed, even yearned for intimacy to fill the emptiness once occupied by the pride of perfection, fear, doubt, anxiety and worry. Though remnants of these sins always lingered near, Love kept them at bay with the flames of His fire.

In my emptiness, Love came. He filled me with Himself. He gave me intimacy with others in ways I had not known. I opened my heart to those around me, revealing the secret parts of me that had been hidden for so long. It all seemed so good. I was beginning to feel full. But all was not completely well. I opened my heart to one who was unable to cherish the contents that lied therein.

He swayed me with his sweet words, his charm, and his sensitivity. He spoke my language, the language of intimate communication. But Love did not give him permission to enter my heart without making a commitment to me and the little girl waiting to be loved there inside.

It felt so good to finally feel cared for by another man. But it wasn't true love. It wasn't refined by the fires of commitment and Love. It was as fleeting as the flirting eye. It was a story not meant to pass on.

The end of that year, I knew pain once more. It entered my heart uninvited and settled there. I cried and spent many days alone, wandering what I had done wrong. I had gotten too intimate, too close to someone who simply *couldn't* love me like I needed to be loved. And so, my heart was grieved. I brought its broken pieces to Love's lap and asked Him to put it all back together again. In my desperation, I allowed another to do for me what only Love could do. Though the price was great, my Love redeemed my broken heart. He taught me His ways, and I grew to know the source of real love again, Love Himself.

No longer empty, but *in* Love.

Healing Balm of Love

"The Lord is near to those who have a broken heart, and saves such as have a contrite spirit"
Psalms 34:18

In the silence of solitude, I looked. But no one could be found. Those who said they loved me, where were they now? It was my sophomore year and I thought that friendship would reap only the sweet fruits of fellowship and intimacy. But, *oh*, there is a bittersweet price to pay for intimacy with the wrong person. I opened my heart and left it unguarded, only to find myself feeling rejected and alone. How did my sweet Love heal His adulterous daughter? I don't even know how He did it, but He did. I walked around campus and at home, my heart aching, like a wound that refuses to close or be healed.

With all that was within me, I had to keep going, keep smiling, keep singing God's praises while I nursed a bleeding heart. *Why* was my love so sensitive, so trusting, so sweet and so intense? I wondered. I felt betrayed when a young man I felt close to told me that he had been physically intimate with one of my girlfriends. It was like I had been openly humiliated, yet in private. I cried even into the summer. I went to the altar and no one was there to comfort me, save God's Holy Spirit; and I learned that He is more than enough.

Soon I realized what Love was doing. He had baptized me with the Holy Spirit just a few months before my heartache. I didn't realize it then, but as I write this I know that Jesus had already healed me at Calvary and His healing was manifested inside of me when I was baptized with the Holy Spirit.

I had allowed a person to fill the empty spaces of my heart. For some people they try to flood their emptiness with alcohol or numb it with drugs or food. For others they fill their void with success, money, material possessions, power, position, prestige. Still, for others they fill the deep chasm of their soul with intimate relationships. Such was my case, until I was filled to overflowing with the Holy Spirit.

My baptism happened at a church meeting during my sophomore year of college one Thursday night. Although I was already saved and indwelled with the Holy Spirit at the moment I accepted Christ, I was not immersed, filled, baptized and overflowing with the Holy Spirit with the evidence of speaking in tongues, until that night! My intense longing for *more* of God led me to stay after the service and go into another room in order to be filled with the Holy Spirit. In this room with my other sisters in Christ, scriptures were read about receiving the Holy Spirit (Acts 1:5, 2:4, 2:39). I received those scriptures as truth both for the early church *and* for me. Then, I began to worship the Lord in prayer. My hallelujahs, hallelujahs, hallelujahs, hallelujahs, hallelujahs, hallelujahs, hallelujahs…became utterances I had never heard come out of my mouth before. I kept saying them until the stream of utterances became a river of utterances flowing forth from my inner most being.

Jesus' answer to my pain was His Spirit and His Word, which came alive to me that night: "but whoever drinks of the water I shall give him will never thirst. But the water that I give him will become in him a fountain of water springing up into everlasting life" John 4:14.

When I returned to school my junior year, I saw the person who once incited pain within me and felt *nothing*. My heart was healed. The feelings and the pain had dissipated like dust on a windy day. Even as I write these words, I feel the healing balm of Love.

When I saw the source of my pain, I didn't feel rejected any longer. *That's* the healing balm of Love: the power of the Holy Spirit. His work is so complete you don't even remember the pain as you once experienced it-permeating your being, your very soul. He gave me hope where I felt none "…and hope does not disappoint, because the love of God has been poured out within our hearts through the Holy Spirit who was given to us" Romans 5:5.

That pain is a past memory, not meant to pass on. That pain is no longer mine because Jesus bore it for me at Calvary, He cleansed me with His blood, and bathed me in the healing balm of His Love: His Spirit.

Never Forsaken by Love

*"For He Himself has said, 'I will never leave you
nor forsake you"
Hebrews 13:5b*

Love reminded me that He would never leave me nor forsake me. In a world where we forget to call one another back, we let months and years go by without visiting one another, and we live our lives like time spent with one another is but a formality, I would rather have Love.

Love made His promise clear to me during the first quarter of my junior year in college. Emotionally exhausted from an intense summer, I felt like I had nothing left to give God, myself, or others. The seed of fear and worry was starting to grow in my heart as I fought with myself, trying to decide if I had chosen the right major.

During this quarter, I felt the closest I had ever felt to losing my mind. My memory felt stripped. It was hard to read, and I struggled not to lose everything I tried to remember. Everyday living was difficult as I tried to figure out what I was "supposed" to be doing. I felt like I wasn't hearing from God because He didn't seem to order my every step. What spiritual bondage I had ascribed to.

During those three months, my thoughts were of evil. I lost the little self-confidence that I had, and I felt that I was paralyzed with nothing to give anyone. And then, yes, Love came.

I was on a plane to New York City for the first time. I had left school afraid to get on a plane alone. I just wanted someone to hold me day by day until my confidence was restored. But, my Love spoke. I don't remember the time, but it was dark, close to the midnight hour. As I sat in the aisle seat, tears fell, streamed down my face. My tears took me unaware, and I couldn't control them. They just came, and I tried to wipe the tears away for fear of looking foolish to the person sitting next to me. But Love, simply yet so powerfully told me that "He loved me."

In my mind, prior to that moment, I saw visions of violence. I thought that others would hate me if I left Stanford only to become a "failure". But Love shattered those demonic visions, and surrounded me with His unfailing love. I felt bereft of anything worthy of love. My worth had always been rooted in what I could do, what I could give to others.

Now, I sat empty-handed and barely able to remember what to do next. It was then, at *that* moment I learned what real Love is. It was *Love* who gave me the very breath I inhaled each day. *Love* gave me my memory. What I knew came from *Love's* supreme wisdom. *Love* was the source of my competency.

All that is good and perfect comes from Love. He healed me on that plane and replaced my visions of violence with visions of love. I am *never* forsaken by Love.

Love Renewed My Mind

*"And do not be conformed to this world, but be
transformed by the renewing of your mind, that you
may prove what is that good and acceptable and
perfect will of God"*
Romans 12:2

"As a man thinketh in his heart, so is he" (Proverbs 23:7).
Those words came to my mind over and over during the first
quarter of my junior year. Why *these* words? I thought about
my thoughts and realized that I was *becoming* what I thought
about. I felt lonely and unloved because that's the way I
thought about myself. My thoughts were reflections of inner
hatred and despair. I became the manifestation of my heart.

Thus, I had the power, by the help of Love through the
anointing of His Spirit to think good thoughts about myself,
instead of evil. As I intentionally chose to read my Bible and
meditate on the words of Love, my healing came. Instead of
trying not to think evil of myself, I learned to focus on Love's

thoughts of me-thoughts of peace and not of evil, His plan to give me a future and hope according to Jeremiah 29:11. I had to wash my mind with the Word of Love, like taking a shower. The renewing of my mind was and still is a *daily* and *continual* process where I have to simply *believe* what Love says about me, and what He thinks about me, as *true*.

My healing did not happen easily or instantly during that season of my life, but with time, Love truly renewed my mind, and ushered me into a season of joy and peace which I had never known before.

The Fruit Love Bore

"No chastening seems to be joyful for the present, but
grievous; nevertheless, afterward it yields the peaceable
fruit of righteousness to those who have been trained by it"
Hebrews 12:11

Chastening. Peaceable fruit. Training. Why do God's children have to suffer? How these questions plagued my soul during my last few years of college. I loved my Lord Jesus, and desired but only to please Him, but the price I had to pay felt almost unbearable.

The answer He spoke to my heart was simple, yet hard to receive. My will had the potential of separating me from the One who died for my soul's redemption. Even with the mask of perfection, I didn't want to praise Jesus or surrender *everything* to His sovereignty, His lordship over me.

My will had to die through the furnace of suffering. To truly *know* Jesus I had to share in the fellowship of His suffering. We all must bear the cross of Love. And so, I bore my cross. I endured through the pain of death to myself.

Yes, I cried. I wept. I felt like parts of me were dying, because they were. I had to release and let go of fleshly ways of thinking and living.

I realized by the enlightenment of the Holy Spirit, that I served other people out of a sense of compulsion. My sense of worth was tied to the amount of good things I could do. Because of His love for me, Jesus helped me to "die" to this way of thinking.

No words can adequately describe my death, but by my Savior's grace, I endured through each painful experience. To what end did I endure my cross? The *peaceable fruit of righteousness.* The peace of being in right standing before God, with God, and in God.

Every moment was worth the joy beyond my cross. I have joy unspeakable and love immeasurable. My circumstances don't matter any longer. The kingdom of God inside of me is greater than the world outside of me. My soul overflows with joy even in the face of rejection and attacks from the enemy of my soul.

My mind has known no greater peace. The love I am abiding in runs deep, saturating my soul with *shalom*- the peace of God. I am no longer shaken by man's inability to love me, or his lack of desire to cherish the beauty that is within me.

The love I am walking in has overtaken my soul, and I can finally love myself. When I think about what Love has done for me, my soul cries "hallelujah!" And, oh, Love shattered the abyss of my loneliness. I used to look up into the sky, and sigh from the depths of a desolate heart. Now, I laugh! I sing! I shout! I rejoice! For the children of a barren woman are more than she who has a husband! The fruit love bore.

Love Made Manifest

In this the love of God was manifested towards us, that
God has sent His only begotten Son into the world, that we
might live through Him"
I John 4:9

When I needed someone to pray for me, Love sent them.

When I needed someone to hold my hand, Love sent them.

When I needed someone to hold me in their arms, Love sent them.

When I needed someone to listen to the cries of my heart, Love sent them.

When I needed someone to warm me with their presence, Love sent them.

When I needed someone to make me laugh, Love sent them.

When I needed someone to feed my hunger, Love sent them.

When I needed someone to dry the tears from my eyes, Love sent them.

When I needed someone to tell me what I needed to hear, Love sent them.

When I needed someone to usher me into God's presence, Love sent them.

When I needed someone to remind me of my hope in Jesus, Love sent them.

When I needed someone to truly care about the me *inside* of me, Love sent them.

Love made manifest.

The Consummation of Love

"And the angel answered and said to her, "The Holy Spirit will come upon you, and the power of the Highest will overshadow you; therefore, also, that Holy One who is to be born will be called the Son of God"
Luke 1:35

Just as Mary was impregnated with Jesus, my Love, I too have been impregnated with the *seed* of God's purposes for my life. Love came into me at the moment I received Him as my Lord and Savior. Love made manifest inside of me in the form of His Holy Spirit, the third Deity in the Holy Trinity on that precious day I was baptized with the Holy Spirit.

Now, the kingdom of God lives in me, moves and breathes inside of me. The visions and dreams which I see every time I close my eyes, remind me that I am pregnant with God's purposes for my being.

This baby growing inside of me must be nourished and cared for, just as I care for my body. I am a temple of the Holy Spirit, and Love is the Creator of my destiny. His divine fingerprints pressing on the womb of my spirit call me to greatness as I walk with Him each day.

Love holds me and gently guides me along as if I were with child. His love transcends a physical touch or the intercourse of the flesh. Our love is spiritual. Our spirits intertwine in sweet communion. I am my Beloved's and He is mine.

He provides for my every need as I carry His seed within me. I am determined to never abort this baby within me, through unbelief, doubt, fear or the lies of satan. By faith, my purpose shall be birthed and my destiny consummated.

Now, I earnestly await and purposefully prepare for my divine delivery date.

The consummation of love.

Waiting on Love

*"Wait on the Lord; Be of good courage, And He shall
strengthen your heart; Wait I say, on the Lord!"*
Psalms 27:14

In the middle of the sowing of a seed and the harvesting
of the fruit it bears, there is a season of waiting. As a senior
in college, I felt as if I was waiting in every area of my life.
Waiting for the moment when I would walk down the aisle to
obtain my degree. I labored for four years to graduate from
college and with each new day I longed to taste the fruit of
completion.

I waited to find out if I had been accepted to the Graduate
program I prepared for an entire year to attend. I waited for a
man to come into my life and recognize my worth, and simply
love me, finally.

I've waited and longed for deeper intimacy with Love.
I've waited for all of my prayers to be answered. I've waited

for my heart to heal again. I've waited for old thoughts and habits to die. Waiting, waiting, waiting.

What do you do, when all you can do is wait? "Wait on the Lord and keep His way, and He shall exalt you to inherit the land" Psalms 37:34.

In all of my times of waiting, I've wished for all of my heart's desire to be immediately manifested, but yet and still I've learned to wait. I've learned to treasure the seasons of waiting which Love takes me through. I've learned that what I've been waiting for is already done, for Jesus finished everything at Calvary.

I can rest deeply in knowing that my life is not mine to control, but God is perfectly in control of all that concerns me. I am free from the burdens that come from obtaining all that I want during my waiting seasons. In those seasons, I can come to *know* the One who waited patiently for me to respond to His call- my Love, Jesus.

Love is the One for whom my soul longs. I seek Him fervently throughout my days. *He* is the One for whom I await. *Love* is my good and expected end.

Waiting on Love.

Love, My Provider

What do I need or desire that Love cannot fulfill? I immediately think about my physical desire to be held. Where's Love when I simply need a hug? He's right there, embracing me with His spirit, satisfying me beyond the momentary fulfillment of a hug.

Where's Love when my burdens seems so heavy that I don't feel like I can take another step? His strength literally carries me in His arms.

Where was Love when my tuition bill was due and I had nothing to give? He provided for *every* financial need I had. Love opened doors to jobs, scholarships, fellowships, internships and provided me with financial blessings beyond what I could even think or ask.

Love has faithfully supplied all of my needs. There is no need that is too deep that God's hand cannot supply. When I look at my life, I can see the unfailing, never ending mark of Love.

My womb is filled with the finest foods. My body is covered in warmth. My mind has found peace with God, myself and others. My closets are overflowing so that I can give away to others.

I am not limited to holding the hand of only one soul, but my tent has been enlarged, and I can hold in my arms, as many as my heart can love. I owe no man anything but to love him and her. I am full-full of hope, joy, peace, and the contentment which only God can give. Who is the Man who provides for me? His name is Jesus and His provision is boundless, unconditional and free. Love, my Provider.

In the Arms of Love

*"He who dwells in the secret place of the Most High shall
abide under the shadow of the Almighty"*
Psalms 91:1

Everyone who has ever held my hands knows that they are cold, even on the hottest summer day. By nature, I am cold and often dream about being enveloped in warmth.

Life has taken me through some very cold moments, only to lead me right back into the arms of Love.

In the arms of Love, He warms my aching coldness with the rays of His Sonlight. His touch and His presence fill me with warmth overflowing. Man can only warm me temporarily, but Love warms the depth of my soul. In Love's arms, I am like a rose in the Master's hand:

"Tattered and torn. Cold.
    Cast away and tossed to and fro in the wind.
        Black spots covering my frail weak frame.

No sweet smelling scent.
No beauty to behold.
Until He came.

A rose in the Master's hand

My Master came.
He touched me with His love.
Through my death, He gave me life.
Light.
The beauty of His Son's light gave
me the power to stand firm on fertile
soil in the dark night.
My enemies came to devour me,
trying to destroy my beauty given by the Master
after setting me free.
But I am not like any rose that sadly tries to
stand, No

I am a rose in the Master's hand

Firmly planted on the Rock of my salvation,
I am no longer a slave to deprivation, but saved
by reconciliation.

His grace waters my soul,
His love pulls the weeds of life which try to
choke away my faith,
His hand gently prunes away the thorns
attached to me,
His presence within me makes me grow.

On Christ the solid rock I stand, for

I am a *rose* in the Master's hand.

The Call of Love

*"I, the Lord have called You in righteousness, And will
hold Your hand; I will keep You and give You as a
covenant to the people, As a light to the Gentiles, To open
blind eyes, To bring out prisoners from the prison, Those
who sit in darkness from the prison house"*
Isaiah 42:6-7

It is not enough for me to receive the love of Jesus. It is not
enough to commune with Him alone. It is not enough for me
to feast on the fruits of His Spirit. I must answer His call-the
call of love. What is this call? "Beloved if God *so* loved us, we
also ought to love one another" I John 4:11.

As I abide in the arms of love, satisfied with His all-
encompassing provision, waiting on Him, carrying the seed of
His purposes for my life, I must *love others* as I love myself.

I must be God's arms extended to the hurting, His heart
opened to the helpless, and His feet willing to rescue those in

trouble. Love must be multiplied over and over again from heart to heart, soul to soul, person to person.

As I answer the call of Love, I strive toward this vision: "To manifest the love of God in Jesus Christ in the lives of young men and young women, so that they will in turn love God, themselves and others."

The call of Love.

Married to Love

"For your Maker is your husband, the Lord Almighty is
His name; And your redeemer is the Holy One of Israel;
He is called the God of the whole earth"
Isaiah 54:5

This last reflection of my journey with Love, I dedicate
to You, Lord Jesus:

"You are the image of the invisible God. You are Love
made flesh. In You exists the fullness of the Holy Trinity-God the
Father, God the Son, and God the Holy Spirit.

You were there when I thought that I would die from the
pain of life. It was Your love poured forth in Your blood shed at
Calvary that saved me. You are my Savior. My sins nailed You
to the cross, but Your love for me kept you there. And now, I am
completely and totally free. Free to love just as You have loved me.

You were there the years I felt desperately alone. Your
presence has walked with me, every moment of every day. Because

of Your love, I am not afraid of silence or quiet moments when the music of life stops, and I must go home and live the life I sing about.

"You are my Friend. As a true Friend who lays down His life for another, You have given me Yourself, and promise to give me even more. Your love overwhelms me, fills me, heals me, over and over and over again.

Your words quicken my spirit with joy, unspeakable joy. You are the Lover of my soul. I am Your beloved, Your bride. I delight to sit in Your shade, for the fruit of Your words are sweet to my taste.

I want You to find me spotless and without blame when You come to take me home.

You are my song.

You are my joy.

You are my peace.

You are my present.

You are my future.

You are my strength.

You are my Love.

Lord Jesus, I choose You, though countless things vow for my love and affection, I am betrothed to You. There is no one else like You.

Our marriage is like a dance. It ebbs and flows from past to present to future, with one single note. The melody of love is the bond of perfection uniting us as bride and Groom.

To the world and all of its inhabitants I make known my undying love for You. I love You with the life that I live.

When I face attacks, rejection, heartache, pain and isolation, I STILL choose You.

For Your hands that were pierced, I give You my hands to touch lives.

For Your head which they crowned with thorns, I give You my mind to renew.

For Your side which they pierced, I give You my womb to bring forth my destiny.

For Your feet which they pierced, I give You my feet to go where You lead me.

I long only to bring You the utmost pleasure. I vow to love others as You have loved me. Lord Jesus, I DO.

Epilogue:

"Love Made Manifest John"

"However, as it is written: No eye has seen, no ear has heard, nor has it entered into the heart of man, what God has prepared for those who love Him. But God has revealed it to us by His Spirit: for the Spirit searches all things, yes, the deep things of God" 1 Corinthians 2:9-10

It was the summer of 2002 and I had walked away from one chapter of my life into a completely new one as a 22 year old college graduate. Though I had been married to Love for 15 of those 22 years and in love with Him with all of my being, there still remained an incompleteness in my soul, a longing in my heart for my husband here on earth: *manifested* in human flesh. I longed for him since I was a little girl. Though I didn't know who he was, he was a part of my spirit which I couldn't shake. I tried to imagine myself alone and happy without him, but I couldn't do it. Though I enjoyed being single, I wanted *more*. I wanted my husband. As time passed, I realized that not only did I want him, I *needed* him.

My faith in Love concerning my husband grew weak, because I had waited for him almost my whole life, and had experienced rejection and disappointment during the wait. I knew Love was *able* to bring my husband to me, but I was beginning to wonder if He *would.* My heart felt so weak during that crossroad in my life. Finally, on July 28, 2002, I came to a place of surrender in my soul and told Love that I would trust Him again to bring my husband to me in His perfect time.

Confined within the limits of my finite mind, I thought His perfect time would be at least a year, so I settled in singleness and found contentment there. I am so glad that Love's thoughts are *higher* than my thoughts and His ways are *higher* than my ways!

I will forever celebrate the day my Love answered me and manifested my husband: August 3, 2002.

John L. Savage Jr. called me on the phone from Hickory, North Carolina while I was laying on my parent's couch in Rocklin, California on *that* day. Not only was I soon lifted up in love with John, but I became in love with *Love* all over again.

A year earlier, in the summer of 2001, the Lord had spoken to me through His Word in Matthew 21:22, saying "And all things, whatsoever you shall ask in prayer, believing you shall receive." At that time, I responded by asking Him in faith for my husband, and for a year my faith was tested.

In the fullness of time, actually a year after I asked for my husband, Love answered the deepest desire of my heart and I came to know again that the Word of Love is true. In that moment, my faith was strengthened and renewed. No longer was I hoping, praying, waiting, and believing, but now I was living my dream, tasting the fruit of my faith and most importantly the faithfulness of Love. Specifically, the word Love gave me in my spirit while I waited to see John became true: "Delight yourself also in the Lord, And He shall give you the desires of your heart" Psalm 37:4.

When Love made manifest John, first I heard his voice, then he entered my heart as my soul received him as my husband, and finally I saw him and our spirits became one when we married in April 2003. We became the manifestation of what Love first conceived in the spirit. Our love unfolded as prophesied in I Corinthians 2:9:

> *"However, as it is written: No eye has seen, no ear has heard, nor has it entered into the heart of man, what God has prepared for those who love Him. But God has revealed it to us by His Spirit: for the Spirit searches all things, yes, the deep things of God"*
> *1 Corinthians 2:9-10*

For the first four months of our love, we never saw each other, in the flesh that is. But the Holy Spirit truly revealed John as my husband and me as his wife. Throughout the whole process, the Holy Spirit was revealing not only more of John to me, but more of Love Himself. Love Himself made manifest to me first in my spirit as my Father, then as my Savior, Redeemer, Crucified and Resurrected Lover, then as my Lord, and finally as the Husband of my soul, from the time I was 7 to the age of 22. Then shortly after turning 22, He made manifest John.

I *heard* who John truly is in his heart every time we talked on the phone, because "A good man out of the good treasure of his heart brings forth good ; and an evil man out of the evil treasure of his heart brings forth evil. For out of the abundance of the heart his mouth speaks" Luke 6:45.

John's very name means "God is gracious, God is good", and John is the manifestation of his name to me in every possible sense of its meaning. Through John, Love has tirelessly fed and nourished my body, given me joy I've never known, comforted my soul in the midst of sorrow, empowered me to face adversity and press past it, and set my spirit free to be all that He created me to be. Most of all, John's love has liberated the little girl inside of me to blossom and thrive upon the fertile soil of his love. In John's love, I have been transformed from a rose to a lily. In John's love, my spirit is free-free to live, free to love, and free to be who God has called me to be: a lady, a lover, a wife, a mother and a minister of the gospel of Jesus Christ.

Now, my story is complete. Though many days lie ahead of me and many more chapters of my story have yet to be lived, my life is already complete. I am loved forever in eternity and loved here in time. I have found Jesus Christ, rny Love and my Lord to be exactly who He says He is: the one and only true and living God, who does not lie. He is a rewarder of those who diligently seek Him (Hebrews 11:6). My life speaks of His faithfulness, the truth of His Word, and the rewards and miracles of a life abounding in Him. Now, as I live my life one day at a time, my greatest desire is for Love to make manifest to me over and over and over again. Love made manifest John.

The Arms of Love are Opened to You...

If you are reading this book and you have never asked Jesus Christ into your heart and asked Him to be your Lord and Savior, now is the time. He stands at the door of your heart, waiting for you to let Him in. Apart from Jesus your sins will keep you from having a deep, personal and intimate relationship with God, the Father. But, with Jesus inside of you and you inside of Him, you can know your Heavenly Father and be at peace with the Creator of your soul, because Jesus took your sins and gave you His righteousness. You simply must believe that Jesus died for your sins and God raised Him from the dead on the third day. Acknowledge Jesus as Lord, and particularly as your Lord, and you will be saved. (Read Romans 10:9-10)

Pray now and ask Jesus into your heart, in your own special way... My greatest joy is to hear from you and the decision you've made this day. Please write me and ask the Holy Spirit to lead you to a Bible-based and Holy Spirit-filled church home where you can grow in the knowledge of God, love God, love others and be loved. Most of all, enjoy every moment of your marriage to Love. Here's a memorial of the decision you've made:

I, _____asked

Jesus Christ to make my heart His home, save me from

my sins and be the Lord of my life on this_____

day of_____, 20____.

Love is praying for you right now (Hebrews 7:25) and I am praying for you too. We love you, Leah & Love

Leah C. Savage has a heart for young ladies and women from all socioeconomic backgrounds to intimately know the love of Jesus Christ. She has worked extensively in the non-profit sector as an intern, consultant, volunteer, teaching fellow, mentor, teacher and workshop facilitator. She has worked with organizations such as NUMI, Little Lights Urban Ministries, and Good Neighbors Child Development Center where she currently serves in an administrative capacity. She is a graduate of Stanford University where she received her B.A. degree in Comparative Studies in Race and Ethnicity. She is known for her excellent speaking abilities and her passion of ministering love, healing and the Word of God to young women. She is also known for her elegant beauty and peaceful spirit. She currently lives in Sacramento, CA with her two beautiful children, Miquela and Elisha and the man of her dreams, John L. Savage Jr.